# EMBRACING A LIFE OF
# MEANING

## *Kathleen Norris*
### *on Discovering What Matters*

A 5-Session Study by Kathleen Norris with Tim Scorer

"A Place on Grand River" and "Gold of Ophir" from *Journey: New and Selected Poems, 1969-1999*, by Kathleen Norris, © 2001. Reprinted by permission of the University of Pittsburgh Press.

The scripture quotations used within (unless otherwise noted) are from the *New Revised Standard Version Bible*. ©1989 by the Division of Christian Education of the National Council of Churches of Christ in the USA. Used by permission.

DVD filmed at St. John's Episcopal Cathedral in Denver, CO. Special thanks to the cathedral staff for their gracious hosting.

Closing prayers by Tim Scorer.

Morehouse Education Resources,
a division of Church Publishing Incorporated
Editorial Offices: 600 Grant Street, Suite 630, Denver, CO 80203

For catalogs and orders call:
1-800-242-1918
*www.ChurchPublishing.org*

*Photos on pages 10, 26, 42, 56, 70* © Copyright 2012 by Jeremy Rau. All rights reserved.

ISBN-13: 978-1-60674-113-9

# TABLE OF CONTENTS

# QUICK GUIDE TO THE HANDBOOK

## TEN things to know as you begin to work with this resource:

### 1. HANDBOOK + WORKBOOK

This handbook is a guide to the group process as well as a workbook for everyone in the group.

### 2. A FIVE-SESSION RESOURCE

Each of the six sessions presents a distinct topic for focused group study and conversation.

### 3. DVD-BASED RESOURCE

The teaching content in each session comes in the form of input by Kathleen Norris and response by members of a small group; just over 30 minutes in length. A DVD Table of Contents is included to enable you to go directly to the beginning of each session.

### 4. EVERYONE GETS EVERYTHING

The handbook addresses everyone in the group, not one group leader. There is no separate "Leader's Guide."

### 5. GROUP FACILITATION

We based this resource on the understanding that someone will be designated as group facilitator for each session. You may choose the same person or a different person for each of the five sessions.

### 6. TIME FLEXIBILITY

Each of the five sessions is flexible and can be between one hour and two or more hours in length.

### 7. BUILD YOUR OWN SESSION

Each of the five sessions offers you four to five OPTIONS for building your own session.

### 8. WITHIN EACH OPTION

Most of the options feature a mixture of quotations from Kathleen Norris and the video participants, plus questions for discussion. Some options also offer additional creative activities.

### 9. BEFORE THE SESSION

Each session opens with five questions for participants to consider as preparation for the session or to consider after the session.

### 10. CLOSING AS IF IT MATTERS

Each session concludes with a prayer written by Tim Scorer specifically for the session.

# BEYOND THE "QUICK GUIDE"

## Helpful information and guidance for anyone using this resource:

## 1. HANDBOOK + WORKBOOK

This handbook is a guide to the group process as well as a workbook for everyone in the group.

- We hope the handbook gives you all the information you need to feel confident in shaping the program to work for you and your fellow group members.
- The work space provided in the handbook encourages you...
  — to respond to leading questions.
  — to write or draw your own reflections.
  — to note the helpful responses of other group members.

## 2. SIX-SESSION RESOURCE

This resource presents Kathleen Norris's insights on meaningful living framed as five distinct topics of study:

1. Belief Matters
2. The Bible Matters
3. Community Matters
4. Place Matters
5. We Matter

## 3. DVD-BASED RESOURCE

The teaching content in each session comes in the form of input by Kathleen Norris and response by members of a small group; just over 30 minutes in length.

Kathleen Norris's warmth, insight and humor stimulate thoughtful and heartfelt conversation among her listeners.

The edited conversations present group sharing that builds on Norris's initial teaching. They are intended to present to you a model of small group interaction that is personal, respectful and engaged.

You will notice that the participants in the DVD group also become our teachers. In many cases, quotes from the group members enrich the teaching component of this resource. This will also happen in your group—you will become teachers for one another.

We hope that the DVD presentations spark conversations about those things that matter most to those who struggle to discover what matters most in the 21st century culture and in their personal lives.

## 4. EVERYONE GETS EVERYTHING

The handbook addresses everyone in the group, not one group leader. There is no separate "Leader's Guide."

- Unlike many small group resources, this one makes no distinction between material for the group facilitator and for the participants. Everyone has it all!
- We believe this empowers you and your fellow group members to share creatively in the leadership.

## 5. GROUP FACILITATION

We designed this for you to designate a group facilitator for each session. It does not have to be the same person for all five sessions, because everyone has all the material. It is, however, essential that you and the other group members are clear about who is facilitating each session. One or two people still have to be responsible for these kind of things:

- making arrangements for the meeting space (see notes on Meeting Space, p. 8)
- setting up the space to be conducive to conversations about the things that matter most
- creating and leading an opening to the session (see notes on Opening, p. 8)
- helping the group decide on which options to focus on in that session
- facilitating the group conversation for that session
- keeping track of the time

- calling the group members to attend to the standards established for the group life (see notes on Group Standards, p. 8)
- creating space in the conversation for all to participate
- keeping the conversation moving along so that the group covers all that it set out to do
- ensuring that time is taken for a satisfying closing to the session
- making sure that everyone is clear about date, location and focus for the next session
- following up with people who missed the session

## 6. TIME FLEXIBILITY

Each of the five sessions is flexible and can be between one hour and two or more hours in length.

We designed this resource for your group to tailor it to fit the space available in the life of the congregation or community using it. That might be Sunday morning for an hour before or after worship, two hours on a weekday evening, or 90 minutes on a weekday morning.

Some groups might decide to spend two sessions on one of the major topics. There's enough material in each of the five topics to do that. Rushing to get through more than the time comfortably allows, results in people not having the opportunity to speak about the things that matter most to them.

## 7. BUILD YOUR OWN SESSION

Each of the five sessions offers you up to seven OPTIONS for building your own session. How will you decide what options to use?

- One or two people might take on the responsibility of shaping the session based on what they think will appeal to the group members. This responsibility could be shared from week to week.
- The group might take time at the end of one session to look ahead and decide on the options they will cover in the next session. This could be time consuming.
- You might decide to do your personal preparation for the session (responding to the five questions), and when everyone comes together for the session, proceed on the basis of what topics interested people the most.

## 8. A FORMAT WITHIN EACH OPTION

Almost every option mixes quotations from the video (from Norris and the other participants), along with thoughtful questions for discussion. Occasionally, options simply feature questions or other creative activities.

## 9. BEFORE OR AFTER THE SESSION

Each session opens with five questions for participants to consider either as they prepare for the session or as they reflect on the session afterward.

- We intend these questions to open in you some aspect of the topic under consideration in the session, which may lead you to feel more confident when addressing this question within the group or in further discussions outside the group.

- Sometimes these questions are the same as ones raised in the context of the session. They offer the opportunity for you to do some personal reflection both before and/or after engaging in the group conversation on that topic.

## 10. CLOSING AS IF IT MATTERS

For each session there is a final prayer written by Tim Scorer to use when closing the session.

- It's important to close well. It's like a period at the end of a sentence. People leave the session ready for whatever comes next.
- Whether you use the closing prayer or something else one of your own choosing, closing well matters.
- Another aspect of closing is evaluation. This is not included in an intentional way in the design of the sessions; however, evaluation is such a natural and satisfying thing to do that it could be included as part of the discipline of closing each session. It's as simple as taking time to respond to these questions:
  — What insights am I taking from this session?
  — What contributed to my learning?
  — What will I do differently as a result of my being here today?

# POINTERS ON FACILITATION

## 1. Meeting Space

- Take time to prepare the space for the group. When people come into a space that has been prepared for them, they trust the hospitality, resulting in a willingness to bring the fullness of themselves into the conversation. Something as simple as playing recorded music as people arrive will contribute to this sense of "a space prepared for you."
- Think about how the space will encourage a spirit of reverence, intimacy and care. Will there be a table in the center of the circle where a candle can be lit each time the group meets? Is there room for other symbols that emerge from the group's life?

## 2. Opening

- In the opening session, take time to go around the circle and introduce yourselves in some way.
- Every time a group comes together again, it takes each member time to feel fully included. Some take longer than others. An important function of facilitation is to help this happen with ease, so people find themselves participating fully in the conversation as soon as possible. We designed these sessions with this in mind. Encouraging people to share in the activity proposed under *Beginning Conversation* is one way of supporting that feeling of inclusion.
- The ritual of opening might include the lighting of a candle, an opening prayer, the singing of a hymn where appropriate, and the naming of each person present.

## 3. Group Standards

- There are basic standards in group life that are helpful to name when a new group begins. Once they are named, you can always come back to them as a point of reference if necessary. Here are two basics:
    — Everything that is said in this group remains in the group. *(confidentiality)*
    — We will begin and end at the time agreed. *(punctuality)*
- Are there any others that you need to name as you begin? Sometimes standards emerge from the life of the group and need to be named when they become evident, otherwise they are just assumed.

# SESSION | 1

## BELIEF MATTERS

### BEFORE THE SESSION

Many participants like to come to the group conversation after considering individually some of the issues that will be raised. The following five reflective activities are intended to open your minds, memories and emotions regarding some aspects of this session's topic. Use the space provided here to note your reflections.

1. Take some time to reflect on your journey of belief. You might find it helpful to draw it on a path on a page, noting times of insight, challenge, fullness, emptiness, hope, gratitude, transformation and so on.

2. Think about the kind of words and writing that are important to you in your believing: hymns, creeds, poems, scripture passages, prayers, graces, psalms, short stories, essays and so on.

3. As you move through the week notice yourself as a believer in a culture that doesn't espouse just one belief system and that is sometimes either cool or even hostile to Christianity. What's it like to be a Christian in this period of North-American history?

4. Think about times in your life when it has made a big difference for you to be a person of faith and belief. Feel the gratitude for those times.

5. Someone comes to you and asks, "What is belief and why does it matter?" What do you say?

The theme of this series is "Embracing a Life of Meaning." You have come together as a group, ready to uncover some responses to this question: What does a life of meaning look like for us as a people of faith in this second decade of the 21st Century?

Even if you have met everyone in the group before, it is still a brand new group taking on a new topic of exploration. Take a few minutes to introduce yourselves in two ways:
• by telling your name
• by telling about something that gives meaning to your life today

In September of 2011, another group met in Denver to learn with Kathleen Norris and to grapple with the same issues that are on your agenda for these five sessions. They will introduce themselves in the same way that you have just done.

 Play the first section of the DVD for Session 1, up until Kathleen begins to talk.

Play the second section of the DVD for Session 1, through Kathleen's talk (about the next 10 minutes).

Here are 20 statements that Kathleen makes in these opening 10 minutes of teaching.

1. The fact that I was singing in church choirs from the time I was four years old probably has more to do with my beliefs—my spiritual development—than any catechism I learned as a teenager.

2. The hymns come before the sermon for a good reason: if we are to become believers we need that immersion into poetry not our ordinary speech, but poetry.

3. The world tells us that what you see is what you get; Christianity denies that: it asks us to look for something more. It points to greater and deeper things, but not necessarily other-worldly things.

4. In my faith I'm encouraged to look for the sacred and holy that is hidden in ordinary life.

5. In media coverage almost all the press is given to the most extreme right-wing Christians so that many people are convinced that is the only form of Christianity.

6. We ourselves resist the counter-cultural nature of Christianity: at it's very heart this religion insists that God is always there for us, loving, forgiving us and welcoming us as we are.

7. Most of us manage to resist the core message of Christianity most of the time.

8. One of the biggest problems we have with the concept of belief today is how illiterate most of us are when it comes to the Bible and Christian tradition.

9. When Jesus is asked who is my neighbor he doesn't give a discourse on the concept of neighbor; he says, "A man was going down from Jerusalem to Jericho when he fell into the hands of robbers." Jesus' storytelling made me feel right at home.

10. To ask, "What do you believe?," is not at all the same as asking, "What do you think?"

11. The verb "to believe" in its origins means "to give your heart to." Belief comes from your whole self and not just your intellect.

12. Belief is not a list of things you know for certain; it's much richer than that and also more subtle. Belief always carries within it the seed of doubt.

13. We need belief more than ever to help us to live together.

14. Worship with all its repetitions and hymns and prayers is meant to fortify our belief and make us feel at home in a community with other people who are also struggling with their own belief.

15. I used to hate creeds, but I have finally come to terms with them. In some ways the Nicene Creed is just the family story we Christians like to tell. In its strange phrases, it's as if we are all speaking in tongues.

16. As a poet I'm used to saying things I don't fully comprehend.

17. What the poet William Stafford said about poetry is also true of prayers and creeds: "Successful people cannot find poems; for you must kneel down and explore for them."

18. The metaphors I use in poems and stories I tell are out there in the world—part of the fabric of the world created by God. I didn't invent them; I only discover or stumble across them.

19. There are things I can do to make myself more receptive to these discoveries: prayer, the practice of silence, trying to avoid distractions and limiting my use of television and the Internet.

20. Belief is simply a matter of paying attention to the world around me, to the little ordinary things that are so easy for me to overlook. They will reward me beautifully if I give my heart to them; if I believe.

Which one of these statements did you find yourself most strongly drawn to? Sit with one other person and make that statement personal to you by speaking about its meaning in your life.

# OPTIONS FOR FURTHER EXPLORATION

Before going on to choose from the following options for conversation and reflection, watch the rest of the DVD for Session 1 in which Kathleen engages with the small group from St. John's Cathedral, Denver.

## OPTION 1: WHAT IS BELIEF?

Kathleen offers four ways of beginning to answer the question about the meaning of belief:

- *The verb "to believe" in its origins means "to give your heart to." Belief comes from your whole self and not just your intellect.*
- *To ask, "What do you believe?", is not at all the same as asking, "What do you think?"*
- *Belief is not a list of things you know for certain; it's much richer than that and also more subtle. Belief always carries within it the seed of doubt.*
- *Belief is simply a matter of paying attention to the world around me, to the little ordinary things that are so easy for me to overlook.*

1. How would you define *belief?*

Encouraged to think of belief as more than a list of things that one knows for certain, the participants in the group talk about the meaning of belief through the lens of their own experiences:

Kim:

> *One of the things I love to share with the young people I work with is that this isn't just something that happens one day and "boom!" that's it, you've got it all. You just keep discovering and keep discovering. The doubts creep in, and you keep wrestling with them. It's a life-long journey. I'm beginning to see as I get older that it gets better. It just keeps getting better and better. That's a little parable in itself!*

Maria:

> *I'm using all the resources I can draw on right now. Becoming a grandmother has been a really true experience. Seeing this new life, this young child and infant; there is such closeness to the Creator! Even without her words; it doesn't matter. With her eyes I can see there is something that the child is showing me that I want to learn about myself because I once had that. I had that. I want to tap into that again.*

2. What moments in your life illustrate how belief is a powerful and very present reality?

3. If you take Kathleen's lead and think of belief as *"simply a matter of paying attention to the world around me, to the little ordinary things that are so easy for me to overlook,"* how does that change the way you experience the world around you?

# OPTION 2: FINDING WORDS WHERE GOD HAS HIDDEN THEM

Kathleen Norris quotes the 19th-Century mathematician, Bernhard Riemann, who said, *"I did not invent those pairs of differential equations. I found them in the world where God had hidden them."* Kathleen encourages us to approach our search for our personal language of belief in the same way. The words are out there as part of the fabric of the world created by God. Our task is to get out there on the search where we will stumble across them. The American poet, William Stafford, said much the same thing about poetry: *"Successful people cannot find poems; for you must kneel down and explore for them."*

The participants in the small group pick up on this idea of taking on the hard work of searching for the words of belief as though God had hidden them out there for them to find. These are some of the ways that each of them talks about the rigor of this personal search for meaningful language:

Amanda:

> *I was raised an Anglican, going to church with my parents, just skimming over the words, barely understanding anything. When I got married I came to the United States. For a while my husband and I went to a Southern Baptist church where he was raised. I sat there. It was just like being in a convention center, not what I was used to — sitting in a church with the tinted windows. I finally found St. John's. I remember when they said, "stand…sit…kneel." I said, "Wow! I'm home!" Then we said the Nicene Creed. O my goodness; it was literally like coming home.*

Kathleen:

> *I'm going to an Episcopal church now. There are some people who will not say the creed. It just bugs them too much. I was there once. I really hated it. I didn't know what it was all about. But after being in church a while, I did think, this is the family story. It's the story you might tell at the family reunion. Of course, there's all this theological history with it, but it's our story. It's the story that the church has chosen to tell for two thousand years. It's not just my story; it's our story. I really am more comfortable with it. I do laugh sometimes when I think of us all speaking in tongues, with no idea of what we're saying, but that's fine.*

Kim:

> *One day my son said to me that what he learned growing up from our church was to hold things open, and that if there were stories that didn't make sense to him to just hold them open and that one day he might find meaning there.*

1. What role do words have in your life of belief and faith? Include in your discussion the place of words in things like hymns, creeds, prayers and relationship with the Bible.

3. What feels like "home" for you today in your worship life? Why do you think it is that place?

2. Have you had that experience of stumbling across words in the world where God seemed to hide them waiting for the right time for you to find them? Talk with someone else about what that was like.

# OPTION 3: LIVING BELIEF IN THE DOMINANT CULTURE

In introducing this topic, Kathleen makes the following points:

- *Christianity is counter-cultural:* The world tells us that what you see is what you get; Christianity denies that: it asks us to look for something more. It points to greater and deeper things, but not necessarily other-worldy things. In my faith I'm encouraged to look for the sacred and holy that is hidden in ordinary life.

- *Because Christianity is counter-cultural the culture reacts to it in very negative ways:* scorn, ridicule, dismissing and ignoring the faith as irrelevant, and anachronistic in the modern world.

- *One of the ways we see Christianity as negated is in media coverage:* almost all the press is given to the most extreme right-wing Christians so that many people are convinced that is the only form of Christianity.

- *We ourselves resist the counter-cultural nature of Christianity:* at it's very heart this religion insists that God is always there for us; loving, forgiving us and welcoming us as we are. Most of us manage to resist the core message of Christianity most of the time.

- *One of the biggest problems we have with the concept of belief today is how illiterate most of us are* when it comes to the Bible and Christian tradition.

1. We find ourselves in a time when it is more likely that we are choosing to be Christian and re-affirming that choice rather than simply being born into it and staying with it. Because of that we are more likely to be identified as people who have made that choice; we are more likely to "stand out" as people who have opted for a religious path. Is that true for you? What difference is this making in the way you live out your faith?

2. Rebecca reflects on a very specific personal way that the dominant secular culture has called her to greater account as she lives out her faith:

> My new husband is a geologist. He was not raised in the church. Before we met he had started going to another church. He is now coming to St. John's; he was baptized here before we got married as his choice. I feel like he is my conscience, my mirror. I can see things through his eyes: "You say you believe this, but why are people acting this way?" He has such a clear lens. He has an idea of how a Christian community should be, but we don't always live up to that. He calls me to be a better person and to live more intentionally. He is someone of great integrity, so he calls me to greater integrity.

3. What are your stories about relationships with people outside Christianity or new to Christianity that illustrate what it's like to live in a time when being Christian calls for a clarity of choice and commitment?

During the conversation, Kathleen observes that we need belief more than ever to help us live together. Belief, seen as a response to the challenges of life, is a gift that is available to us in moments of crisis or over the long process of personal growth and development.

Kathleen leads us to consider the gifts that belief can bring when she reflects on the movement away from the fear and self-consciousness of our teens and twenties:

> *When you start to shed the self-consciousness and the fear you had as adolescents and young adults—maybe the tradition you were raised in was very strict and you're leaving that and not too sure of yourself—when you start to get free from fear, you find it really does get better and is a process in which you are growing without fear. That's one of the great gifts belief can bring.*

Kim builds on this from her own experience of a ministry with young people:

> *I think that in every session we talk about what faith really is; we talk about words like* trust *and* beloved. *I'm always telling them about the idea that this is a journey, and that right now in their lives they're in a place where they're all about themselves— all about finding out who they are— differentiating from their parents. What I often see as they come back from one or two years in college is that they're starting to look for something else, something more. So we talk about the "More"; the more of God and Jesus in our lives.*

And Margaret reflects on the gift of belief and practice in a time of deep loss and grief:

> *Ten years ago our 18-year-old grandson, who was a freshman in college, died suddenly in his sleep of a ruptured aorta. One moment he was here and vital; the next he was gone. That evening at 5 o'clock I sat down to do my centering prayer. It never occurred to me not to, because that's what I do. And I felt myself rocked. It you observed me you probably wouldn't have seen me moving, but I was rocked and that continued for the journey to the funeral. I kept wondering how is my family getting by without centering because I just knew that God was present with me. It wasn't God who took Chris. Chris died. God was holding me like a child, not like a grieving grandmother.*

What are the gifts you have received that you would consider "gifts of believing?"

## OPTION 5: BELIEF AS JOURNEY

Believing is a life-long dynamic process. To tell the story of your believing is to pull out from the narrative of your life one of its most powerful themes. What would you include in the telling of your belief story up to this point in your life? Here are some of the ways Margaret tells her story:

>*I realize that my beliefs change everyday. I was raised a Southern Baptist and I was in that for 25 years where belief was everything. Then I moved into the congregational faith where the emphasis was more on living than believing. But it wasn't until I began meditating 37 years ago that I became open to allowing myself to be changed in every moment of everyday. It's still happening. Something new comes along and I ask myself, "Am I being here now, present, and living from that place?" For me it takes an hour of centering prayer a day to stay there.*

>*I've been an Episcopalian for 22 years and it's feeding my soul. But I look back to my Baptist roots when I learned the Bible: I memorized so that now I can recite whole passages. I can bring up whole passages so I feel such gratitude for that. At the same time I'm studying Kabbalah and I'm understanding Jesus more than I ever have in the Christian church because I'm getting the mysticism and I'm coming to love him in a new way. So, everything is gift even though at the time you leave it, thinking, "I'm moving on!"*

>*My shaping began after I retired from psychotherapy practice and was led into becoming a spiritual director. The people I've seen over these years are of different faiths and some agnostic. I have been challenged to watch me language so that I'm open to everyone. What I finally got was to see people as Jesus sees people. What a challenge! So eventually what people got from me was respect and love.*

The underlined words are the kind of words and phrases that people use in telling the stories of their lives. You might use one or two of them as starting points in speaking about your own journey of belief. For example: *My shaping began after I* _____ *and was led into* _____.

In telling the stories of our believing, there is power in doing that together in a group, but you may not have the time to do that in a regular session. You do have the option of taking a whole extra session to hear one another's stories of belief and faith. It's a remarkably affirming process!

In a regular session you might just tell one part of your story of belief to one other person, just to get a sense of what it's like to have your story witnessed by another.

## OPTION 6: (PERSONAL REFLECTION)

Following the session you will continue to think about issues raised both on the DVD and in your small group. This suggestion for journaling is offered to support you in continuing your reflection beyond the session time.

In your journal note the current season of the church year (Advent, Christmas, Epiphany, Lent, The Season after Easter, Pentecost, The Season of Creation [where that is named]). Choose from these stems as ways of beginning your daily writing about your journey of belief in this season:

> I notice how this season colors the way that I live my faith…

> In this season of the church year, belief matters to me in these ways…

> As I continue to embrace a life of meaning, I discover the meanings this season has in my life…

# CLOSING

Offer this prayer:

> Blessings on this life,
> birther of meaning.
> Blessings on these people,
> companions on the Way.
> Blessings on this day,
> light of the Beloved.
> Blessings on the past,
> stories of belief.
> Blessings on our voices,
> holy conversation.
> Blessings on our departure,
> promise of return.

# SESSION | 2

## THE BIBLE MATTERS

### BEFORE THE SESSION

Many participants like to come to the group conversation after considering individually some of the issues that will be raised. The following five reflective activities are intended to open your minds, memories and emotions regarding some aspects of this session's topic. Use the space provided here to note your reflections.

1. Go around your home and find any Bibles that are there. Take each one off the shelf and recall, as you are able, how it came to you, what stories you associate with it, and times when it has been important to you. Tell someone about it.

2. Open a Bible to a passage that matters to you. During the day take time now and again to reflect on that passage, allowing its words to wash over you and to evoke thoughts and feelings in response to it.

3. Turn to Genesis chapters 6–9 and read the story of Noah and the Ark. What memories of this story do you have from childhood? What meaning does it hold for you now? See if you can find information from books, a scholar or the Internet about the origins of this story and the meaning it might have had in the context of the time when it was first written.

4. Read through any book of the Bible, pausing as you go to reflect not only on the impact of the text on you, but also on the intention of the writer in committing these words to papyrus, hide, parchment, clay or stone.

5. Ask friends, acquaintances and family members about why the Bible matters—or does not matter—to them.

## GROUP LIFE

This is the second meeting of the group. There is already a sense of membership carried over from the first session; but there's a good chance there may be people attending for the first time. Make sure everyone is introduced and welcomed.

You might take a few moments for a check-in on the theme of the session: *The Bible Matters*. For example, each person might name one way that the Bible is important to them.

This is a quick 30-second check-in, not a time for lengthy storytelling! That will come later in the course of the session.

# ESSENTIAL: KATHLEEN NORRIS ON WHY THE BIBLE MATTERS

Play section 1 of the DVD for Session 2, through Kathleen's teaching—about the first 12 minutes.

In this time of teaching, Kathleen is very clear about why the Bible matters to her. Here are five key points that she includes in these opening 12 minutes. For each point, take four minutes in conversation with one other person to respond briefly to the point that Kathleen is making. After four minutes change to another partner to respond to point #2, so that in 20 minutes you will have had conversation with five other people on five different issues.

1. The Bible is a mirror where we find our own lives truthfully reflected. Sometimes we may not like what we see, but we can still experience the essential wisdom it offers for our living.

2. We are often repelled by what we read in the Bible, but for all its violence, genocide and political abuse, we can still see it as being an accurate reflection of human behavior in our world today.

3. People of all sorts and conditions are sustained in their living and find meaning for their lives through a practice of Bible reading. It's amazing how I can open the Bible and begin reading and very soon find something that addresses the reality of my life at that moment.

4. The Bible is experienced very differently at the various stages of our lives. The stories and verses we learned in childhood—and turned away from as young adults—may sink in and stay with us waiting for a time later in life when we are ready for them and need them.

5. Our culture doesn't really have much use for the Bible. People generally know two to three sentences of the Bible and that's it. The idea of reading all the way to the end of the Revelation of John in order to experience its resolution is alien to most people.

# OPTIONS FOR FURTHER EXPLORATION

Before going on to choose from the following options for conversation and reflection, watch the rest of the DVD for Session 2, in which Kathleen engages with the small group from St. John's Cathedral, Denver: Rebecca, Margaret, Amanda, Kim, Maria and Tim (the facilitator).

## OPTION 1: HOW THE BIBLE SUSTAINS US

In her opening teaching, Kathleen says that for many people the Bible sustains their lives. She goes on to say that whether or not you have a deep understanding of it, whether or not you know Hebrew or Greek, none of that really matters; you can read the Bible with a very simple faith and it has great meaning.

The small group participants pick up on this theme and offer these stories from their own relationship with the Bible:

Margaret:

*I love the way I can read a passage of scripture and it can tie I with something right now. This summer I was introduced to a book called, Do You QuantumThink? (by Dianne Collins). I told my friend in California that I do not"get" physics, but she insisted so I starting reading it and realized that it was very powerful and rich for me today. I began to listen to some lectures on the web. One day I read in this passage in Isaiah 43: "I am about to do a new thing; now it springs forth, do you not perceive it? I will make a way in the wilderness and rivers in the desert" (Isaiah 43:19). I was so excited that I emailed the author of the book and quoted this whole thing. I said that I was so alive with the material (in her book). She emailed me back within an hour and said, "I am Jewish. I'm on my way to visit my mother and I'm taking this passage to her about all you say*

*about my work. That was written hundreds of years ago: I'm about to do a new thing. This was a new thing for me!*

Amanda on a hard time in her life when the Bible made the difference:

*For a long time I went to a Dominican Convent. We had religious studies but I barely understood what these passages were talking about. It was drummed into us. Even through college, I didn't open the Bible. Then when I met my husband, he would go to his church with his Bible in tow. It was so hard being a newly married person and coming to a new country. We were older—both in our late 30's. I remember one time we were sitting on the bed. We felt so defeated. He sat on the bed and opened the Bible. I snapped, "Now what are you looking at?" As he was going through Psalms, he just found something. He said, "Come and read this." I did. I think that's when I thought, "OK, we've got to make this work. I'm here. I'm not going anywhere. This is what I've chosen." Sometimes just opening the Bible and reading gives you the strength to carry on.*

Rebecca's humorous story about her relationship with her mother:

> I had an experience several years ago when my parents came out here to visit and I was in a hard place—grumbling and complaining. I just felt like the adolescent daughter from growing up—out of sorts. On their last evening they came with me to do evening prayer before I took them to the train. I don't remember what the psalms were, but afterwards my mother said, "See, that's exactly what you need to hear and I've been trying to tell you the whole time I've been here, and there it was in the psalm!"

What stories do you bring to the group about ways that the Bible has sustained you and brought meaning to your life? Share those with one another as time allows.

# OPTION 2: BIBLE AS A MIRROR

Kathleen introduces this theme in this way:

> *I think of the Bible as a mirror: we can find our own lives reflected there. But it's hard for us to like this mirror. It doesn't reflect us as we would like to be. The Bible tells us the truth about human beings: how we treat each other, how we relate to God. Often, like Moses and the prophets, we try to wiggle out of our responsibilities, our call, maybe trying to bargain with God.*

Margaret later offers an example of this dynamic in her own life:

> *A number of years ago a president was elected who was very difficult for me to accept, so I sat down to do Lectio\* because I was so mad. The passage I read had this line: "Pray for the leader." I said, "O, no, no, no; anything but that!" But I did make a commitment and I did pray for a good six months for this person whom I detested.*

Tim asks:

> *Were you changed, Margaret, by the discipline of praying for that leader?*

Margaret:

> *Of course. I came to love the person. I disliked everything about him, but I came to see him as human. I tried to be less judgmental. Yes, I was changed. It wasn't just that I had to. It's like praying for Gaddafi; we're called to pray.*

Kathleen:

> *You can always pray that people come to their senses! The Bible pushes us in these directions that are quite uncomfortable.*

Margaret:

> *Praying for their highest good. That in turn makes me pray for the highest good of the nation and wakes me up out of my petty little political efforts.*

\*Lectio Divina, or Praying the Scriptures, is a spiritual discipline in which someone reads a chosen scripture passage seeking a word or phrase for that moment and then meditating and praying on it, all with the intention of hearing the word that God has for them at that time.

Listen to Psalm 73 being read aloud (p. 33). Be attentive for any phrase or line that seems to be holding a mirror up for you.

An Asaph Psalm

1-5 No doubt about it! God is good — good to
    good people, good to the good-hearted.
But I nearly missed it,
    missed seeing his goodness.
I was looking the other way,
    looking up to the people
At the top,
    envying the wicked who have it made,
Who have nothing to worry about,
    not a care in the whole wide world.

6-10 Pretentious with arrogance,
    they wear the latest fashions in violence,
Pampered and overfed,
    decked out in silk bows of silliness.
They jeer, using words to kill;
    they bully their way with words.
They're full of hot air,
    loudmouths disturbing the peace.
People actually listen to them—can you
      believe it?
    Like thirsty puppies, they lap up their words.

11-14 What's going on here? Is God out to lunch?
    Nobody's tending the store.
The wicked get by with everything;
    they have it made, piling up riches.
I've been stupid to play by the rules;
    what has it gotten me?
A long run of bad luck, that's what—
    a slap in the face every time I walk out the
      door.

5-20 If I'd have given in and talked like this,
    I would have betrayed your dear children.
Still, when I tried to figure it out,
    all I got was a splitting headache...

Until I entered the sanctuary of God.
    Then I saw the whole picture:
The slippery road you've put them on,
    with a final crash in a ditch of delusions.
In the blink of an eye, disaster!
    A blind curve in the dark, and—nightmare!
We wake up and rub our eyes... Nothing.
    There's nothing to them. And there never
      was.

21-24 When I was beleaguered and bitter,
    totally consumed by envy,
I was totally ignorant, a dumb ox
    in your very presence.
I'm still in your presence,
    but you've taken my hand.
You wisely and tenderly lead me,
    and then you bless me.

25-28 You're all I want in heaven!
    You're all I want on earth!
When my skin sags and my bones get brittle,
    GOD is rock-firm and faithful.
Look! Those who left you are falling apart!
    Deserters, they'll never be heard from
      again.
But I'm in the very presence of GOD—
    oh, how refreshing it is!
I've made Lord GOD my home.
    GOD, I'm telling the world what you do!

Share with one another in the group a way that
this psalm invites you to see the reflection of
your own life and living.

Kathleen talks metaphorically of the Bible as a mirror; but later on in the conversation some of the group members talk about the physical reality of some of the Bibles in their lives:

Kim tells this amazing story:

> *My Bible represents my journey because I got it when I was confirmed in another church; it has my name in gold on it. I went through my teen years really having a crisis of faith, and then my mother died when I was 21. It wasn't until I was in my early 30s that I came to the Episcopal church. I started getting involved in Christian education.*
>
> *My neighbor from my growing up years just called me out of the blue one day. We were talking about our faith journeys and at some point I said, "You know, Fritz, the one thing I wish I had back is my Bible," and he said to me, "O, I have it! Your mother gave it to me before she died. She said you'd ask for it back one day."*

And Maria reflects thoughtfully on the beauty and significance of her Spanish Bible:

> *It's so good to have such a book; to have it and hold it with me. It goes to the heart! My Bible is 50 years old. It was a gift when I was a teenager. I really treasure this book. It is in Spanish. I have it in a beautiful lined case that I made for it. It sits on a wood and gold lectern. It really touches my soul when I go to open it. It has become my friend: this book of consolation; this book of joy; this book of illumination. The more I read it in Spanish, the more I feel strength.*

What are the stories of *your* Bibles?

Right at the beginning of the group discussion Rebecca plunges into the challenging question of what to do with the dark texts in the Bible:

*I was just talking to a father of a young child who's wondering how to read Bible stories with his son, especially the story of Noah. It's one of our favorite stories for kids because of the animals. You can make it cute and sentimental, but what kind of sadistic God creates these people and loves them and then wants to kill them all? How do you teach that story? I didn't really have an answer. I'm still thinking about it, especially as someone who has a responsibility for teaching Bible stories.*

Kathleen proposes a way of dealing with such texts that honors both child and adult:

*I think you can let the children play with the story when they're young. Let the dad worry about the deeper things. Give the child a Noah's Ark and let him play with it!*

*I was just reminded of a medieval woodcut I saw. It came from the years after the plague. There was a woodcut of the Ark and Noah on it and the corpses of all the dead animals who hadn't made it into the Ark on the ground. Of course, in that culture at that time they were trying to figure out where this plague had come from. Scientifically they had no idea why this devastation had happened, but somehow it was a sign of hope that there was an Ark and that Noah was there. There were live animals and there was a live person there with all the corpses of animals and people on the ground. Every*

*culture in every age might find a way to come to this story.*

*I think you have to be age appropriate with Bible stuff. One of my grandmothers use to scare me by saying all kinds of crazy things like this: "Jesus will come as a thief in the night!" Not real helpful when you're five years old!*

And Kim speaks from her experience with Godly Play and the Story of Noah:

*Over the years of doing Godly Play with children and with the adults who were teaching, this kind of question has come up a lot. We talk about how we're telling the stories of the People of God's experience of God. As I think about all of these dark questions I think of God setting us free and how we are co-creators with God.*

*One of the places in the story of Noah in Godly Play that I like is when you're holding the Ark up above everybody's head and talking about how everywhere they looked there was water. You say, "But God did not forget Noah and the creatures on the Ark and sent the sun to dry up the rain." And you talk about the goodness of God and God's blessing on them. I think about that a lot when I talk to people about those really hard times. God can come into anything and transform it; but God also allows us to do all the things we do and allows the cycles of our living to go on and on.*

1. Rebecca clearly presents her concern about the Noah story, and Kathleen and Kim both respond. What do you think of their responses? Would those responses satisfy you if you were Rebecca? What other experience and wisdom would you like to offer to Rebecca, Kathleen and Kim on this matter?

2. What new insights do you have about the Bible as a result of this discussion?

## OPTION 5: BIBLE IN CONTEXT

Several times in the conversation the matter of *context* comes up.

Sometimes the word *context* refers to the context of the lives of the people who are reading the Bible, such as Ephraim, a man from Syria, who was present in worship with Kathleen when a psalm that makes reference to violence on the streets is being read. Ephraim's presence leads Kathleen to reflect on the way that social and political context makes a huge difference in our reading of scripture.

Sometimes the word *context* refers to the context of the lives of the people in the Bible. In addition to the story of Noah to which we have already referred, Kathleen talks about the story of the sacrifice of Isaac. We hear her describe how much she dislikes reading this story, but then we hear her reflect on the deeper meaning of the story in the context of the time in which it was written:

> *That is a story against human sacrifice in a culture in which children were often sacrificed. This is a radical story because God is saying, "No, you don't have to sacrifice your children." So it actually has a very positive message, but only if you understand even a little bit about the context in which people would have heard it originally.*

1. When has the context of your life made a difference to the way read or heard a Bible passage?

2. When has a passage come to life and made more sense for you because you have learned something of the context from which that passage came?

3. What are some ways that we can be ever more attentive to the context in which these ancient texts were conceived and recorded?

Kathleen talks about the influence of the Benedictine order in opening the Bible to her in a new and deeper way:

> *I find it ironic that for me as someone raised in Protestant churches that it took exposure to the worship of Roman Catholic Benedictine monks and nuns to allow me to really experience the Bible in a new and more complete way and also helped me to an adult understanding of my faith.*

> *In their daily worship, Benedictine men and women read the Bible aloud and hear it read aloud, allowing the words of the Bible to wash over them, day in, day out, several times a day. In the morning, at noon, in the evening they will gather to recite psalms together out loud and then listen to a portion of scripture. Typically, they will read through an entire book of the Bible in this way. Hearing many of the books of the Bible read out loud reminded me of what a pleasure it is. Most of us aren't read to as adults; it is still a great pleasure. You hear things when you're being read to that you don't find when you're reading by yourself.*

Kim also talks about alternative ways of presentation that can bring Biblical stories to life:

> *When I was growing up I would hear these stories but they were all about dry, dusty, ancient people. They had nothing to do with me. As I started to tell the stories through Godly Play and ask questions about where people found themselves in the story, suddenly I had an experience of it that I'd never had before. This now leads me to a different way of reading the Bible when I do open up the text to read. It sends me further into it and leaves me wanting to read the commentaries and other people's sermons.*

You may have noticed that other members of the small group with Kathleen also talked about ways of engaging the Bible so that it really matters to them.

What are some of the ways that you, as a group, would recommend people trying in order to deepen their experience of the Bible? Four are suggested; can you list another seven?

1. Read through an entire book of the Bible together, hearing different people read as you go, and talking about what you learned from the experience when you are done.

2. Ask someone with experience in the practice of Lectio Divina (Praying the Scriptures) to lead you in an introductory workshop.

3. Have an extra session in which each member of the group introduces the passage of scripture which has the most meaning for them personally.

4. Begin a personal study of the passages of scripture given for each Sunday of the year by going to *www.lectionarypage.net/* and following the directions given there.

5.

6.

7.

8.

9.

10.

## OPTION 7 (PERSONAL REFLECTION)

Following the session you will continue to think about issues raised both on the DVD and in your small group. This suggestion for journaling is offered to support you in continuing your reflection beyond the session time.

Use the following lines from Psalm 139 as starting points for your journal reflection. Write the chosen line at the top of your journal page and then continue for about 500 words, allowing the words of the psalmist to take you into insights that Spirit has for you this day.

1. *You search out my path and my lying down, and are acquainted with all my ways (v. 3).*

2. *Where can I go from your spirit? Or where can I flee from your presence (v. 7)?*

3. *If I say, "Surely the darkness shall cover me, and the light around me become night," even the darkness is not dark to you; the night is as bright as the day, for darkness is as light to you (vv. 11-12).*

4. *My frame was not hidden from you, when I was being made in secret, intricately woven in the depths of the earth (v. 15).*

5. *Search me, O God, and know my heart; test me and know my thoughts (v. 23).*

# CLOSING

Offer this prayer:

> Blessings on our words,
> Word from the Beginning.
> Blessings on our imaginations,
> contracting with Mystery.
> Blessings on the ancestors,
> recorders of revelation.
> Blessings on our voices,
> holy conversation.
> Blessings on our stories,
> great Author of our lives.
> Blessings on our departure,
> promise of return.

# SESSION | 3

## COMMUNITY MATTERS

### BEFORE THE SESSION

Many participants like to come to the group conversation after considering individually some of the issues that will be raised. The following five reflective activities are intended to open your minds, memories and emotions regarding some aspects of this session's topic. Use the space provided here to note your reflections.

1. Stand back from the life of your congregation and notice the gifts that you receive there because of your membership and participation. Give thanks for that.

2. In current writing about congregational life, authors and consultants are unanimous about the importance of hospitality and welcome being extended to those who are visiting, attending for the first time, or seeking a faith home. Note how well your congregation is doing in this regard. Plan to go to another place of worship to experience an alternative expression of hospitality.

3. Matthew reports Jesus as saying, "'For where two or three are gathered in my name, I am there among them" (Matthew 18:20). Pay attention at times when you are meeting with others who are disciples of Jesus noticing when you have a sense of a holy Presence there with you. What difference does it make when you are aware of that presence in the group?

4. What meaning does your participation in community bring to your life?

5. Choose someone in your congregational community who is different from you in at least three of these ways: education, income level, age, ethnicity, gender, sexual orientation, mobility, primary occupation and family life. Invite them to spend time with you in conversation, perhaps over tea or coffee. Tell them that your interest is to get to know someone from your faith community who you perceive to be quite different from you. See what happens when you meet.

## GROUP LIFE

This is the third meeting of the group and the focus this time is on community. Perhaps you are beginning to get a sense of the identity of this particular community of learners. Make sure everyone is introduced and welcomed.

You might take a few moments for a check-in on the theme of the session: *Community Matters*. One way to do that would be for each person to name one community that is important to them in the church and one that is important outside the church.

Play the first section of the DVD for Session 3, though Kathleen's initial teaching, about the first 10 minutes.

In the course of her initial 10 minutes of teaching, Kathleen either quotes others or offers memorable quotes herself. The collection of those quotable quotes sums up the main themes of her opening presentation:

- "For where two or three are gathered in my name, I am there among them" (Matthew 18:20).
- It's not about you, just you!
- You mean, I'm not the centre of the universe!
- I'd like to welcome you to the Body of Christ.
- "I won't belong to any organization that would have me as a member" (Groucho Marx).
- Only God would be crazy enough to bring this group together!
- The only hypocrite I need to worry about on Sunday morning is myself.
- Well, if you don't want to be part of organized religion, just join a church.
- Church is a body, not a trade union or club!
- We've got to keep this church pure!
- We're all just ordinary flawed people who gather because we need to be reminded that God made us and accepts us and loves us and wants us to share that love with others.

Choose one of these quotes that attracts you and talk with one other person about the way it highlights something about community that is important to you.

# OPTIONS FOR FURTHER EXPLORATION

Before going on to choose from the following options for conversation and reflection, watch the rest of the DVD for Session 3 in which Kathleen engages with the small group from St. John's Cathedral, Denver: Rebecca, Margaret, Amanda, Kim, Maria and Tim (the facilitator).

## OPTION 1: FINDING THE WAY INTO COMMUNITY

We heard Kathleen talk about her arrival in a church community at a time when some members of the congregation had been attacking the pastors who were a clergy couple. She realized that God had quite the sense of humor to have her joining a church in the midst of such bad behavior! She wondered what she had got herself into when she was greeted by a head elder of the church who said to her as he awkwardly looked at his shoes, "I'd like to welcome you to the body of Christ."

Margaret remembers her arrival at St. John's Cathedral 22 years before:

*The denomination my husband and I had been involved in, which I still greatly respect, just wasn't filling me at a spiritual level. And someone told me there's a beautiful church downtown that has wonderful music that might feed your soul. I remember walking in one Sunday and just being overwhelmed with the beauty, the color, the procession and the harmony. My soul loves ritual and up to that moment I didn't know it. It was a warm and welcoming community. When I began to connect here, my husband decided to stay at my former church so I was coming in as a woman alone. So I introduced myself to everyone everywhere including in the restroom. I was so welcomed!*

And Amanda talks about the gift of a cathedral community for her as an immigrant feeling lonely for something familiar:

*I actually Googled the word cathedral because I had always gone to a cathedral. I just walked in and thought, "Wow; this is just what I wanted!" The ritual, as I said earlier—stand, sit, kneel—I like that—and the people. The Dean was right there greeting us and making us feel at home. I have had two children baptized here. My husband is never around because he works out of state, so the church has become my community, my support system. People like Kim and Rebecca are like a family I look forward to seeing on Sundays.*

As a staff person at the Cathedral, Kim reflects on the need of young parents to have a place on Sunday morning just to meet and talk over coffee and donuts.

*When we were meeting to organize this, I offered to bring to the group a question as a conversation-starter. The woman who was chairing the organizing committee looked at me and said, "I don't want to hurt your feelings, but what we want is community, Kim; we just want to talk, and get to know one another. If you bring a question I don't think I'd come back the next time." I got what they were talking about. People did get to know one another and then began to talk about some things that they might want from me as Christian educator—things they would like to do together. A whole lot of things came out of that, but it all started with the building of community.*

1. What are your stories of arriving in a congregation?

2. What has kept you coming back faithfully for whatever time that has been?

3. From the stories on the DVD and from your own stories, what are some of the ways that congregations can make connections to "seekers" in a way that connects and keeps them coming back?

4. Kathleen told us of the elder at the church who met her with this sacred greeting, "I'd like to welcome you to the body of Christ." What exactly does that greeting mean when you hear it?

# OPTION 2: THESE PEOPLE: MY PEOPLE

In this option we are focusing on the community experiences of just one member of the group: Rebecca. You heard her a couple of times on the DVD talking about the joys and challenges she faces as a leader in St. John's Cathedral:

*I think that church is one of the last places for intergenerational connectedness. Families don't live together like they used to, so I really appreciate what church offers. I'm not going to have my own kids, but here is a church full of children which is great because I'm far away from my nieces and nephews.*

*Before seminary and before I became a priest, I worked in social action and community organizing. I was around people who thought the same way I did and we were all working together on the same things. As a priest I have to be a priest to people who think differently than I do. I still have to find a place of authenticity and contact to be a priest. I didn't want to go to a church where everybody was like me.*

*My grandmother was an older Anglican. She did not like to pass the peace in worship: "You don't go to church to touch people and talk to people. You go for communion and you talk outside." I had been ordained before she died. One day she said to me, "Rebecca, when you're with the people at your church who are older—more like me—more conservative, remember how much we love each other." I carry that with me.*

*As a priest I've preached at weddings and I've always highlighted the part where the gathered community promises to support these two persons in marriage with their "We will." You have to be married in a public context: your family and your friends and the people who are going to support you in whatever your family looks like. So I told Rick when we got married it was going to be at the Cathedral because this is my community and everyone has to be invited. This is the community that made me a priest. This is my extended family and I had to have them at the wedding. We had no idea how many people that would be. We just opened it up and put up a tent on the lawn and everybody came outside after the ceremony. It was a glorious event of community.*

*The way Rick has been enfolded and accepted and welcomed and loved has been phenomenal. It has opened up for me what my marriage means and what community means: people living committed lives together as a model for community. It was a joyous time of community for us and I think for all the people there.*

1. What are the places in Rebecca's stories that ring true for you? What experiences of church community do you have that are like those?

3. Rebecca talks of her congregation as her extended family. What words and expressions do you use to describe your relationship with your congregation?

2. Rebecca says, "I still have to find a place of authenticity and contact to be a priest." This is something that all people of faith would have to say whether priest or lay person. When has it been challenging for you to be your authentic self in community?

4. What have been the times in your congregational experience when you have deeply appreciated the power and gift of community?

## OPTION 3: PEOPLE ARE USED TO WHAT THEY ARE USED TO!

In her opening teaching, Kathleen made reference to the issue of diversity in community and raised the provocative question, "Who is welcome in the Christian community?" She notes a number of places where the issue of diversity has been visible in Christian history and in the modern church:

- Each of the four gospels has a different view of Jesus and his ministry.
- The epistles were addressed to very diverse communities, from Corinth to Ephesus.
- The movement that Jesus began was a reform movement within Judaism and then became diversified with the conversion of people who were not Jews.
- In our own time we have seen how the presence and role of women and gays/lesbians in the church community has been contested.

Members of the group have their own reflections on diversity based on their personal experiences:

Kim introduces us to a small group that comes together and shares a meal and does centering prayer and Lectio Divina:

*One of the men comes from an evangelical background. So when we look at the scripture and being to have conversation about it, he often has such a different take on it that he opens it up for me in a way I wouldn't have thought of on my own. That's part of the gift of community. You first learn to love one another and then you can really hear one another. You may not agree but you can hear one another. It's true dialogue.*

And Maria acknowledges what a tough question this is for her as a Latino woman in a mostly white congregation:

*I come to Denver from being involved in a community with Latinos, a few blocks from the White House. It is a vibrant community where the issue of integrating the Latinos is a tough reality. It is a shelter, a sacred haven, for many people who are so-called "illegal." So they come and they find hope, protection and prayers. It is something you can call a revolutionary place. I must say I miss that. I'm a Latina, a minority, a woman, so I long for people like me, my color. The Cathedral is in an area where there are not many Latinos. It's a demographic, economic, social and racial issue.*

Amanda also speaks on diversity from the perspective of an African woman from a colonized culture now in the United States as member of a visible minority:

*I came to the Episcopal Church from a background in South and Central Africa where the British colonized us and therefore the Anglican Church. My sister's husband was from Angola and so they were Catholic. Coming to the United States, I was now Episcopalian so I came to the Cathedral where I met a handful of West Indians who were also colonized by the British. I'm not going to meet a lot of people of African descent in this church; you just don't find it. Culturally, it's something you have to have been accustomed to, grown up with. People are used to what they are used to. You don't find major diversity at the Cathedral, but we are all embraced. We feel like a family. We don't think about it in the sense that we are a minority. We are all here for a common purpose, so I feel comfortable.*

Kathleen concludes the conversation:

*There is an entity called the Christian church which contains within it a lot of diversity. Frankly, a lot of diversity makes a lot of people uncomfortable. We want to be with people of our own kind, our own sort. Somehow there's that stability. We're seeking a little comfort level there. We're challenged by diversity and sometimes forget it's really part of the Christian tradition. It's nothing new.*

1.  Who is welcome in your church? Who is not welcome?

2.  What are you not willing to have changed in your church in the name of accommodating diversity? This would be a time to talk about some of the harder issues to confront such as the full and open acceptance of gay and lesbian people.

3.  At another place in the conversation Kathleen says, *"When people say, 'that's not traditional Christianity,' they are often talking about what was traditional for their parents and grandparents—what they were raised in. They have a very narrow view of the church. The early churches of Christianity were incredibly diverse; it was not a monolithic early church."* In what ways have you moved beyond the Christianity that you inherited from your parents and grandparents so that you are not limited in your faith practice by what was traditional for an earlier generation?

4.  What are the challenges your congregation faces in its journey toward this vision as articulated by Kathleen: *"The church is the place where all should be made to feel at home, educated or not, wealthy or poor—all just ordinary, flawed people who gather because they need to be reminded that God made us and accepts us and loves us and wants us to share that love with others."?*

## OPTION 4: THE GIFTS OF COMMUNITY

As you listen to the DVD conversations and teaching you will hear people identifying the ways that community is gift:

• a place where a lonely woman comes and experiences the blessing of friendship and acknowledgement after a chance encounter with a stranger on a plane

• a place which provides opportunity for the expression of two key emotions: praise and lament

• a place where we are reminded that God made us, accepts us, and loves us

• a place where we can put our meanings up against other people's meanings and appreciate something we might have otherwise dismissed as unimportant

• a place where people who have experienced loss of many kinds—a job, a child, a spouse, a marriage, a death—can offer compassionate understanding rooted in their own experience to others who are newly experiencing loss

How has community been gift to you?

At the beginning of her presentation, Kathleen says that if we take the scriptures to heart, we will hear them shouting to us over and over again, "It's not about you, just you!" She notes that one purpose of all great religions of the world is to deflate our egocentricity and deflect our selfishness so that we can devote our energies to serving others. This is a challenge for us in North America where the culture is so concerned with individual rights and needs. Narcisists make good consumers, she observes; they are good for the economy.

Kathleen tells us how she joined a church at the time the church had been attacking the pastors, a clergy couple. There had been secret meetings, hate mail, and ugly rumors, misbehavior so serious that even life-long friends in the congregation had stopped speaking to each other. Kathleen notes that this church was repeating a pattern of negative behavior that had been going on for years, namely booting out pastors as a response to turmoil. When churches repeat this kind of scapegoating of pastors, you know that the issues run way deeper than problems with two ministers. Sometimes it's just too hard for a community to confront its own pathology.

In the previous session on the Bible, Kathleen spoke about how the Bible can act as a mirror for us both individually and communally. Kathleen begins this session by quoting Jesus' words from Matthew 18:20: "For where two or three are gathered in my name, I am there among them." In times when negative behavior is disrupting the life of a congregation and preventing members from recognizing the presence of Jesus in their midst, what to do? We want community. We acknowledge and celebrate the gifts of community, but it takes all the wisdom and skill that community members can muster to establish, build and sustain community life in a healthy way.

What are the "Best Practices" that you have learned as a congregation over the years that ensure that you stay healthy, living out the best of community life as the body of Christ?

## OPTION 6 (PERSONAL REFLECTION)

Following the session you will continue to think about issues raised both on the DVD and in your small group. This suggestion for journaling is offered to support you in continuing your reflection beyond the session time. It's called an *acrostic*. Take a lined page and write the 16 letters of the two words COMMUNITY MATTERS in a vertical line down the left-hand margin of the paper. These 16 letters will now become the first 16 letters of a 16-line free-form poem that you will write on this paper. You know that a line has come to an end when you come to a word whose initial letter is the same as the letter at the beginning of the next line of the poem. So, for example:

**C**hurch hasn't always been my choice
**O**f a place to build relationships that really
**M**atter

    and so on....

Offer this prayer:

> Blessings on our hearts,
> wellsprings of truth.
> Blessings on our words,
> breath-borne connectors.
> Blessings on our intentions,
> love songs to the universe.
> Blessings on our coming,
> community's assurance.
> Blessings on our colors,
> creation's celebration.
> Blessings on our departure,
> promise of return.

# SESSION 4

## PLACE MATTERS

### BEFORE THE SESSION

Many participants like to come to the group conversation after considering individually some of the issues that will be raised. The following five reflective activities are intended to open your minds, memories and emotions regarding some aspects of this session's topic. Use the space provided here to note your reflections.

1.  What places matter to you? Find objects, images, sensate items and people that remind you of some of those places.

2.  Remember a time when you were displaced in some way—a physical move, a great loss, an involvement in a catastrophic event, a profound change in your life—and recall the way that you lived through that and found a new place where there were new meanings that deepened your awareness of things. If you have time to tell someone about this, do so.

3. If you have a place where you worship regularly, go there when it's quiet and you are alone. Sit in that place and imagine all the voices, the songs and hymns, the prayers and liturgies that have been received by that sanctuary. Feel the way that community has been held by that place. Recall the ways that people have reached out from this sanctuary to live out their discipleship in the community all around. Give thanks for all this.

4. Read the poem, *A Place on Grand River*, by Kathleen Norris that you will find in option 5 (p. 68). Sit with its images, its story and its insights. Notice the meaning it has for you today.

5. Take a large sheet of paper and draw a map of your life, noting especially the movement between stability and change, between settling and journeying, between homing and wandering. Notice all the meanings that the word *place* has had for you in your life. Consider whether you want to share this map with anyone else. Follow your instinct.

## GROUP LIFE

This is the fourth meeting of the group and the focus this time is on place. As you connect in community once again, take a moment to remember names and also to enter the theme by sharing with one another how faith communities have been important places to you.

## ESSENTIAL: KATHLEEN NORRIS ON WHY PLACE MATTERS

Play section 1 of the DVD for Session 4, through Kathleen's teaching.

Here are 10 statements that Kathleen makes in this segment. Following each statement is a simple question. Choose one of the statements that appeals to you today and answer its question either in the small group or with one other person. You might have two or three paired conversations, each one with a different statement/question, as a way of helping you all sink into the theme of the session.

1. We are placed in families, towns or cities, cultures, religions, social situations, and traditions.
   *Where were you placed? What difference did it make that you were placed there?*

2. In North-American culture, we have the opportunity to pick up from one place and move on to another one that promises to improve our lot in some way.
   *When have you done that? Did it fulfill the promise? Say more about that.*

3. The ancient monastic tradition of the Benedictines, through their vows of stability and conversion, calls us to see the wisdom of balance between stability and mobility.
   *When have you been aware of living a balance between stability and conversion?*

4. We live in that tension between a routine we can depend on and our restless attraction to the adventure of change.
   *In what ways do you feel that tension right now?*

5. Human beings do need stability. Think of what home means to you.
   *What is home for you?*

6. Encounters with others who have a clear sense of their place in the scheme of things can bring us up short and call us to a renewed search for our place.
   *Tell us about someone who you appreciate for their clear sense of having a place in the scheme of things.*

7. When it comes to change we more easily let go of dated concepts in geography and math than of the faith we learned in Sunday School.
   *How has that been true for you?*

8. Christian faith will always co-exist with heresy because it keeps the dialogue lively, figuring out what works and what doesn't.
   *What heretical ideas have you valued for their capacity to keep the dialogue lively?*

9. Dogma is beauty. Learning that helped me reject both the right-wing fundamentalist Christians and the left-wing atheists who were denying me my place in the faith.
   *In what ways would you say that your place on the spectrum of religious belief is a place of beauty?*

10. When I know my place I can stand up to people who otherwise would intimidate me and knock me out of my rightful inheritance.
    *When have you recently stood up and claimed your place with authority?*

# OPTIONS FOR FURTHER EXPLORATION

Before going on to choose from the following options for conversation and reflection, watch the rest of the DVD for Session 4 in which Kathleen engages with the small group from St. John's Cathedral, Denver: Rebecca, Margaret, Amanda, Kim, Maria and Tim (the facilitator).

## OPTION 1: DISPLACED

The group conversation begins with Maria speaking very movingly and poetically about the experience of being displaced:

> *Place*
> *    I think I've been displaced.*
> *After such an uprooting: coming 1800 miles*
> *from my place of more than three decades.*
> *    I feel uprooted.*
> *So the words* place *and* home *really get me*
> *    to take deep breaths*
> *    until I make myself a home.*
> *I had been able, by the Grace of God,*
> *    to home myself always*
> *    in the midst of all my learning experiences.*
> *After divorce:*
> *    how can you undo 30 years of marriage?*
> *Losing a marriage of 30 years was a death.*
> *I had to embrace death.*
> *Again, by the Grace of God, I homed myself;*
> *    I found home again.*
> *Now here I am in another time of finding home.*
> *Even finding a place to live has become a challenge.*
> *Where do I find a place called* house—casa—home?
> *Here I am again*
> *    trusting that within me there is the light*
> *    that has always guided me—*
> *finding home.*
> *I'm still in the process:*
> *    I've found the Wilderness worship.*
> *    I've found Rebecca and Kim.*
> *    I've found this church—*
> *home already.*
> *Place.*

Margaret, Kim and Rebecca pick up on Maria's reflections and add their own thoughts about displacement and what it takes to live through such a time:

- the way that a dream can provide grounding in a time of displacement
- the way that feeling accepted can be a place to stand in a time of being displaced
- the way that saying "Yes" when asked, "Am I safe here?" responds to displacement

1. When have you felt displaced?

2. What are ways that one can use to respond to the experience of being displaced?

3. What insights have emerged for you from living this five-stage cycle at various times in your life: *placed — displaced — wilderness — homing — re-placed?*

## OPTION 2: DEEPENING INTO PLACE

Kathleen raises the challenge of accompanying people in the process of deepening their faith life in the *place* where they find themselves at any moment:

> *I run into so many people who basically know of the Bible and Christian theology what they got when they were six years old. They really haven't gone beyond that. In order for them to belong to the place they are they have to be invited to learn more of whatever they're ready for: history, theology, all sorts of things that will really help make it a more meaningful part of their lives.*

Rebecca offers a concrete example of this in the teaching of the Catechumenate that requires of participants a rigor and focus that they seize onto in spite of the busyness of their lives. And Kathleen further reflects on the way that religion seems to have been walled off as though there is nothing more to learn. When people begin to taste the possibilities beyond the wall, they want to learn more and more.

1. What has enabled you to deepen into your faith so that it has become a *place* where you feel confident and grounded as you continue to search and grow?

2. What are your learning interests and desires at the present time? How do you intend to pursue those? What can you put in place to support you in that process of deepening?

Kim moves us into a thoughtful consideration of sacred building as place and the role of our buildings in our spiritual journeys.

> *I keep thinking about the word* place *as we're here in the Cathedral. I keep thinking about those stone arches and stained glass windows. I'm going through a struggle in my own mind thinking about the physical space. Is it really that important? I have to say that it is for me. I think the idea that something is dedicated to all this—to have meaning in life and to share it with others—I think there's something incredible about that.*

> *I was in England at Winchester Cathedral and our choir was singing. I heard their voices and I thought about their voices soaking into the stone. I think about the Cathedral here and all the prayers that have soaked into the stones and windows. Everything. All of it.*

And then Kathleen takes Kim's reflection and puts into words the other side of the struggle that Kim had hinted at:

> *How hard it would be to let it go, if it burned down. You'd have the memories and the history. I was just thinking of All Angels Episcopal Church in New York City (www.allangelschurch.com). They had a beautiful, very old building on West End Avenue. I used to admire it as I walked by. Well, in the late 1970s they decided the church was just way too much upkeep. They couldn't maintain it the way it should have been maintained so they gave up three of their four buildings and are now located on the second floor of a nondescript building. Some of the pieces of the church are actually in the Metropolitan Museum of Art. They were able to devote so much more time, energy and money to feeding and helping the poor and to social programs. Of course, the membership shot way up.*

> *Place can become an idol. With beautiful worship space it's tempting to let that happen. I was very inspired by their story and what they were doing, having given up their place and then making a place and home for all these displaced people.*

Rebecca, Kathleen, Amanda and Kim add their voices to the reflection about the tension between sacred space and simple discipleship:

- A giant stone edifice in the middle of the city can be intimidating to strangers who don't know that inside there is an incredible community ready to welcome them.
- A way of testing the effectiveness of ministry that is located in one place is to as the question, "What would the neighborhood miss if we weren't here?"
- A building like this Cathedral can be a place for a group like the displaced Sudanese community to come together for worship and for their own sense of place and home.

1. How do you live the balance between having a sacred space for your faith community without losing the primary focus of your ministry: "to bring good news to the poor. to proclaim release to the captive and recovery of sight to the blind, and to let the oppressed go free" (Luke 4:18). How well are you doing as a community at living this balance?

2. What have been your "Winchester Cathedral experiences" that have fed your spirit in such a way that you have been empowered for the kind of transformative ministry that Kim describes throughout these sessions?

3. Why might the attendance at All Angels Church in NYC have increased so dramatically following the surrender of those three buildings? What other helpful stories do you know of changed congregational relationship with buildings?

# OPTION 4: THE VOWS OF STABILITY AND CONVERSION

In 1986 Kathleen became an oblate, or associate, of a Benedictine monastery, Assumption Abbey in North Dakota. Subsequently, she spent two years in residence at the Ecumenical (now Collegeville) Institute at St. John's Abbey in Collegeville, Minnesota. Her book, *The Cloister Walk*, is structured as a diary of her monastic experience. In her teaching she frequently makes reference to the experience and learning that came from that time in her life. We heard her speak about one aspect of Benedictine wisdom in this session:

> *The ancient monastic wisdom of the Benedictines has something to offer us. While recognizing that people need both stability and mobility, they also need some balance between them. There are two vows of monastic profession that are unique to the Benedictine Order: one is the Vow of Stability in which you promise to remain in this particular community, in this place, for the rest of your life; the other is a Vow of Conversion, of change. It means promising that you will remain open to change, open to conversation and dialogue with others that might have the effect of changing you, converting you, forcing you to change your opinion, change the way that you do or see things. The goals of these seemingly contradictory vows is to make you more balanced in your approach to life and also to the needs of your community.*

The dynamic and life-affirming tension between stability and conversion is reflected in other pairs of words that Kathleen introduces in the teaching that opens this session:

Stability—Conversion
Remain—Move on
Home—Journey
Stay—Change
Stagnant—Mobile
Maintain—Shakeup
Tradition—Rootless
Dogma—Heresy

1. In what ways are you living the authority of these two vows in your life right now?

3. Kathleen talks about the "lively dialogue" that arises in our lives between our need to be both stable and mobile, both staying and changing. In what ways do you see that creative tension being the source of growth in your own life and in the life of your faith community?

2. Which of the two polarities has been more familiar to you in your adult life? Are you leaning more toward *home* or to *journey* at the moment?

## OPTION 5: YOUR OWN BEST SECRET PLACE

When I asked the group members to name a place that matters to them and to which they would like to take us, the diversity of responses was considerable:

Maria would take us to the treatment room where she works as an acupuncturist and to the Wilderness Worship at 6 PM on a Sunday evening at the Cathedral in Denver.

Kim would take us to a special place on Lake Michigan where for years her family has been gathering with other dear friends of all ages for Thanksgiving.

Kathleen would have us go slowly to Assumption Abbey in Richardton, N. Dakota where this huge 100-year-old building rises prominently out of a sea of land so that you can see for 25 miles from the refectory windows.

Amanda would welcome us in the kitchen back in her parent's house in Johannesburg, South Africa, where she would have us sit around the table where so much conversation has been shared.

Margaret wants us to go with her to Snowmass Benedictine Monastery in Colorado, not so much for the buildings but the space and the grounds where stillness is palpable.

And Rebecca would have us travel to the Abbey community on the Island of Iona in Scotland where she first went with school children from the inner city of London 30 years ago, and returned last summer.

Kathleen is not only a teacher and an essayist, but also a poet. Here is one of her poems from the period 1974–1981, in which she celebrates a particular place, giving great attention to detail:

## A Place on Grand River

*You took me once to your place on the Grand:*
*the first log house*
*your father made: the one-room stone,*
*the two-story frame.*
*They flooded out, except the last,*
*built on higher ground.*

*You were the boy in the attic.*
*Your bed was still there, the patchwork quilt*
*half-rotten. You could still pick out*
*your first vest, and one of your mother's dresses.*
*I watched you rage through the rooms,*
*turning things over,*
*working like a thief, growing manic.*

*You pocketed a whetstone.*
*In the kitchen, china plates*
*were set*
*as if someone were returning.*
*You said: we sold it, up and left,*
*moved to town, bought plastic dishes.*
*What year was that? You didn't recall.*
*You were fourteen. Nineteen-sixty. Sixty-one.*

*We made our way in waist-high grass*
*to a ruin of cars, corn pickers,*
*tools. Things you could have used.*
*There'd been a buckboard. Antique collectors got*
*    the wheels.*
*There's no use now, you said.*
*We stood a while in the bitter loveliness:*
*cottonwoods, a turn of the river,*
*hard-won fields, abandoned. In big, swimming*
*    motions*
*we returned to where we'd come through the*
*    fence.*

*I know it seems a lot.*
*The ghosts are in things*
*you've had to steal back: your grandmother's*
*    cast-iron griddle,*
*your father's whetstone. My fields are mostly gone*
*to asphalt and tract houses.*
*Jim, we were lucky*
*other ways, on childhood's holy ground.*
*You got*
*animal timing, I got a way of saying things:*
*nothing is ever lost.*

—*Journey, New and Selected Poems, 1969–1999*,
Kathleen Norris, University of Pittsburgh Press, 2001,
page 39

Choose a special place to which you would gladly take the members of your group. In telling about it pay as much attention to detail as Kathleen does in her lovely poem.

## OPTION 6 (PERSONAL REFLECTION)

Following the session you will continue to think about issues raised both on the DVD and in your small group. This suggestion for journaling is offered to support you in continuing your reflection beyond the session time.

In your journal write the opening words of Kathleen's poem:

*You took me once to your place…*

Continue to write freely (either poetry or prose) about a place that someone once took you and about the meaning that had for you. Don't be concerned about accuracy; this is for your personal exploration of place as you continue to embrace a life of meaning.

## CLOSING

Offer this prayer:

> Blessings on our restlessness,
> source of growth.
> Blessings on our resilience,
> seeing us home.
> Blessings on our sanctuary,
> vibrant with prayer.
> Blessings on our memories,
> mapping our meaning.
> Blessings on our journeys,
> circling back to You.
> Blessings on our departure,
> promise of return.

# SESSION | 5

## WE MATTER

### BEFORE THE SESSION

Many participants like to come to the group conversation after considering individually some of the issues that will be raised. The following five reflective activities are intended to open your minds, memories and emotions regarding some aspects of this session's topic. Use the space provided here to note your reflections.

1. Take your favorite newspaper and go through it noticing how we matter to one another. For example: we matter as entertainment, we matter as income, we matter as life celebration, and so on.

2. Now go through the newspaper wearing the eyes of *God*. How do we matter to God?

3. As you move through your community this week, notice who is visible and who is invisible. What makes them so?

4. There's a poem by Kathleen in Option #5: Gold of Ophir (p. 79). You will hear Kathleen read this poem at the end of the recorded group session. Sometimes it helps to sit with a poem ahead of discussing it, to get your own sense of what the poet is saying. Take time to read the poem several times and consider what Kathleen is saying in it.

5. Here are three things that Kathleen says of God: *God is always seeking us and never abandons us. God is here with us now and we may not know it. God is suffering right along with us, praying for us.* As you go through the week, carry these three assertions with you, being attentive to the difference it makes to embrace them.

# GROUP LIFE

This is the final meeting of the group. Rather than thinking about building your learning community, you are naturally thinking about ending it and reflecting with gratitude on what it has meant for you all to be together in these five sessions. And so we end on the theme, *We Matter*:

When we come together in small groups like this and focus on the real stuff of our lives,
     we know we matter.

When we share a keen anticipation of the time we will spend together in holy conversation,
     we know we matter.

When we spin out the narratives of our lives in the safety of an intentional learning group,
     we know we matter.

When we carry a significance in one another's lives in the days between our meetings,
     we know we matter.

When we regret the ending of the life of our five-session learning group,
     we know we matter.

When we anticipate and initiate future learning opportunities in community,
     we know we matter.

## ESSENTIAL: KATHLEEN NORRIS ON WHY WE MATTER

Play the first section of the DVD for Session 5, through Kathleen's initial teaching.

In her teaching in this session, Kathleen Norris offers us insight into her own theology:

*We matter to God and as such we are a holy people, friends of God, beloved of God.*

*Because we were created in the image of God, it is the here and now that we need to account for.*

*Because we matter to God we have freedom to choose and to change.*

*God is always seeking us and never abandons us.*

*God is here with us now and we may not know it.*

*God is suffering right along with us, praying for us.*

*To be perfect as God is perfect means to be complete, entire and full-grown, willing to serve others.*

*The path to a just society begins with us.*

*Our challenge is to see that all people matter to God whether we like them or not.*

*The scriptures reveal a God in Jesus who is our model.*

*The sacred love that Jesus embodied is present in us here and now.*

*Mary, like every mother, had the courage and bravery to bear a child that would one day die. This is a sign of hope.*

1. How does it feel to you to matter to God in the way that Kathleen presents?

2. Which of these theological statements carry special significance for you? Why is that?

3. What questions come up for you as you read Kathleen's list of what matters to her?

**Note:** In her teaching, Norris makes reference to a Rumanian philosopher and essayist, Emil M. Cioran (1911–1995). For more information on his life and philosophy go to *http://en.wikipedia.org/wiki/Emil_Cioran.*

# OPTIONS FOR FURTHER EXPLORATION

Before going on to choose from the following options for conversation and reflection, watch the rest of the DVD for Session 5, in which Kathleen engages with the small group from St. John's Cathedral, Denver: Rebecca, Margaret, Amanda, Kim, Maria and Tim (the facilitator).

## OPTION 1: BEING AN EXPRESSION OF GOD

In the opening reflection in this section, Margaret offers several ways of thinking about our presence with God in Creation that underscore how we matter:

- From her reading of the book, *The God Instinct* by Jesse Bering, Margaret quotes: "You're not *in* a relationship with God; you *are* a relationship with God."

- Further, she says, "I'm not God, but I am that relationship manifest."

- She recounts an experience she had in a men's medium security prison where she was facilitating a centering prayer group with eight to 10 men. The fact that she, a woman, would sit in the circle of men and close her eyes for 20 minutes, led one of the men to tell her that he had become aware of God's presence in that place.

- Through that incident Margaret declares her intent: "I was expressing God."

- Margaret shares with us three lines of a poem she was saying as she drove into the church that morning:

  *"Think through me thoughts of God,*
  *my Creator,*
  *Quiet me 'til in Thy presence hushed,*
  *I think my thoughts with Thee."*

  She uses such contemplative lines as a way of making the separation between herself and God less and less.

- Margaret reflects on how different this experience of God is from when she was a child and "God was out there somewhere."

1. Margaret, through experience, practice and reflection, has come to an awareness of how she matters. It's clear to her that God can be "made known" through what she does, through the choices she makes. That is really the source of her "mattering." How is this like your understanding of the way you matter?

2. What life stories—like Margaret's story of leading centering prayer in prison—would you tell to illustrate the way you matter in God's unfolding Creation?

3. What spiritual practices, like Margaret's repeating of the three lines of poetry (a mantra), do you follow as a way of deepening the sense of being a relationship with God.

# OPTION 2: TURNING ON THE LIGHT

Maria tells us about her acupuncture practice especially with addictive people:

*I say "the light is off," so my task as an acupuncturist has been to turn on the light. It sounds mechanical but it is not: it is a privilege, an honour, a blessing. I worked for 10 years in DC in this field and every time there was truly a spark of divine light that was in the room when this person was able to say, "You know what? I can sleep. I feel it. I smell it. My bowels move. I'm thirsty. And I don't crave any substance." I really wanted to jump for joy every time I heard that… Now in Denver I'm working with pregnant women. That's where I'm in the presence of the spark of divine light. I know I matter and my message is "you matter; we all matter."*

Kim also tells of times when she has witnessed the "turning on of the light." In her case it was in relation to the homeless people in the neighborhood around the cathedral in Denver:

*A few years ago one of the homeless came to talk to the youth at the cathedral. He said that the biggest gift you can give homeless people is the gift of making them feel they're not invisible; look them in the eye and talk with them.*

Kim reminds us that people feel invisible for all kinds of reasons and that we can all participate in the practice of acknowledgement, one way of "turning on the light" and making an unseen person visible.

1. When have you felt invisible—as though you didn't matter?

2. What happened that made you visible once again?

3. When have you noticed yourself "turning on the light" to ensure another's visibility?

4. What are the forces in our culture that render people invisible?

5. Where are people being made visible in spite of our culture's tendency to do the very opposite?

## OPTION 3: BEING A BLESSING

Rebecca leads us into some reflection on how we are changed by the acts of acknowledgement that we initiate:

> When I'm not feeling good, when I'm distracted, busy and feeling frantic, I don't recognize others. When I notice this about myself, in check-out line for example, and when I take the time to talk to the other person who is checking out my things and have an actual, authentic engagement, I feel better and it changes me. I have an intention that draws me out from my protected, hard place. It is acknowledging it in myself as well as in the other person. When I get distracted, being busy, mean, then I have to change—turn around.

Kathleen picks up the theme by noting this line from Psalm 16:

> Blessed indeed the heritage that falls to me.

She offers this thought: that being mature and whole means being able to say this line from the psalm and mean it. Whatever comes as your inheritance—whether joy or loss, whether good or not—that thing is a given from which you are to make meaning. She continues:

> One of the most profound experiences I had of any psalm was in hearing that line and realizing what it meant. What I was really saying with that line was that whatever comes it is blessed; it's blessed by God and it's my job to make it a blessing in my own living no matter how hard that might be. It might be a tragedy or a loss but I can still find some meaning in there to help me go on.

1. This might be the hardest of all teachings to come to terms with: that you have both the power and the opportunity to turn whatever comes your way, whether in a supermarket check-out or in a family tragedy, into a blessing for yourself and for those you encounter. What experiences have you had of this in your own life?

3. There is a vocabulary for the kind of spiritual practice that is named in this option. These are some of the words that belong in a practice that is about "being a blessing" in the world: *acknowledgement, bearing witness, staying present with an open heart, giving blessings* and *opening to guidance.* Share with members of the group one way that you might sharpen and deepen your practice of "being a blessing" wherever you are.

2. In what way does this insight underscore the theme of this session: *We Matter?*

# OPTION 4: EMBRACING A LIFE OF MEANING

At the end of this five-part series, *Embracing a Life of Meaning*, it would be good to take time to stand back from the five sessions and to talk about the meaning that this experience has had for you and for your group. On the DVD you will hear the five group members who met with Kathleen Norris doing just that.

*Rebecca* speaks of the renewal and hopefulness that has emerged for her in the conversations at a difficult time for her professionally.

*Maria* has found this experience a chance to recollect who she is in the midst of a major life transition.

*Margaret* has come to a place of peace in these conversations following a three-year struggle with the Christian church. She sees more clearly the gifts she has been given through membership in many churches; gifts that balance some of the frustration she feels when Christianity focuses on much about Jesus that doesn't really matter and misses seeing his words through the lens of his identity as a Jewish mystic.

*Amanda* has come to an even deeper realization of the significance of her membership in this faith community where she and her children feel loved and supported in a way they do no where else.

*Kim* underscores her ongoing amazement at how a small group of people meeting time and again can build a circle of trust which can uncover so much more meaning in a text than is possible for an individual to achieve alone.

1. What has this group experience and study process meant to you?

2. How might you take these new insights and build on them?

3. What other topics would you be interested to address in a similar format?

Kathleen chooses to end the series with one of her poems titled "Gold of Ophir." She tells us that the reference is to Psalm 45, a wedding psalm which describes a bride dressed in the gold of Ophir, a fabulous ancient city of unknown location that was renowned for its gold.

She has chosen this poem because it speaks of finding meaning and hope in a grim situation, and finding possibility in a place where you might not see it with your own eyes, but where you do after a nudge from God.

### Gold of Ophir

My heart overflows with noble words…
                    —Psalm 45

*In the dawn, homing*
*nighthawks pass*
*a pale sliver of moon*
*on the rise.*

*A horse snorts*
*in the near-dark,*
*a killdeer keens, a meadowlark*
*embellishes the air*

*and the sun,*

*thunderous silence,*
*touches trees and rooftops*
*with gold.*

*Barefoot in the morning chill,*
*my neighbor stands smoking*
*on her back porch, teenager*
*with a newborn,*
*the father in jail.*

*Bewildered, proud,*
*dazzled by new passion,*
*she takes me in*
*and shows me her daughter,*
*who sleeps grandly,*
*like a queen.*

> —*Journey, New and Selected Poems, 1969–1999,*
> Kathleen Norris, University of Pittsburgh Press, 2001,
> page 72

What are the places and situations where you have, contrary to all expectation, found meaning?

## OPTION 6 (PERSONAL REFLECTION)

Following the session you will continue to think about issues raised both on the DVD and in your small group. This suggestion for journaling is offered to support you in continuing your reflection beyond the session time.

You set out to embrace more deeply a life of meaning. Kathleen chose to approach the task of teaching with reference to five things that matter:

- *Belief Matters*
- *The Bible Matters*
- *Community Matters*
- *Place Matters*
- *We Matter*

She might have chosen any number of things that matter in the business of making meaning in life. What five things would you choose? Use your journal as a place of exploration for this. Take five pages, one for each, and write at the top of each page one thing that matters to you.

Use the rest of the page as a space to explore how that thing matters to you.

## CLOSING

Offer this prayer:

Blessings on our living,
the matter of God.
Blessings on these friends,
holy companions.
Blessings on our stories,
sacred memory.
Blessings on all that comes,
stretching us to the future.
Blessings on our meaning,
evolutionary unfolding.
Blessings on our departure,
promise of return.